A Beginner's Guide to Reading Gregorian Chant Notation

Noel Jones

D1740449

Index

Appendix

Sample Chant Pages

Second Edition

ISBN: 1438257481

©2008 Frog Music Press

To my aunt
Mary Jones,
who has always
encouraged me.

The Musica Sacra website at www.musicasacra.com has a long list of chant book resources that may be downloaded on the internet. They also are publishing and reprinting books on the subject. Their "An Idiot's Guide to Square Notes" by Arlene Oost-Zinner and Jeffrey Tucker is not to be missed.

This short book is an effort to quickly outline and explain the simple system of writing and reading chant. Prior to organization of the writing of chant into this form there were squiggled signs above words that were the first attempts to preserve the oral tradition of sung chant.

We hope that this book serves to answer questions, give you confidence and encourages you to study further the music of the Church.

The next two pages are an overview. You may skip them and go straight on learning to read basic chant on page 4.

A Brief Overview of Chant Notation

- The foundation of modern written music notation

- Easier to read than modern notation

- Takes less space on the page than modern notation.

- Chant is made up of small groupings of organized notes

- Each group has a different and consistent purpose

- Music staff covers just the range of the human voice

- There are only four lines in the staff

- Notes are always directly above the vowel that is sung

- There are only two clef signs

- There is only one sign, a flat. that alters the pitch of a note

- All chant may be written with the same note, a neume

- Neume groupings organize notes over their word syllables

Sample

1. An Alleluia written using the basic chant neume, a simple note for each pitch.

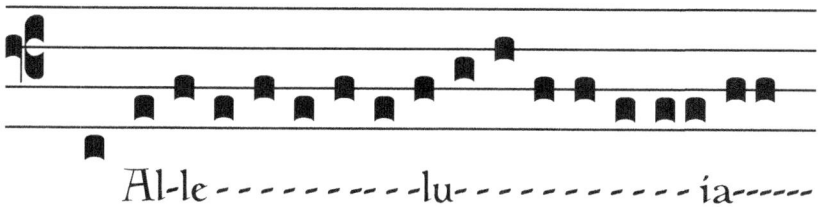

Al-le --------- -lu----------- ia------

2. This Alleluia using chant neumes that clearly show the grouping of pitches above the syllable being sung, as well as interpretation...

Alle-   lu-   ia

3 The same Alleluia using in modern notation. Note the amount of space this takes, a major issue when writing on expensive vellum in medieval times. Chant notation is compact and to the point.

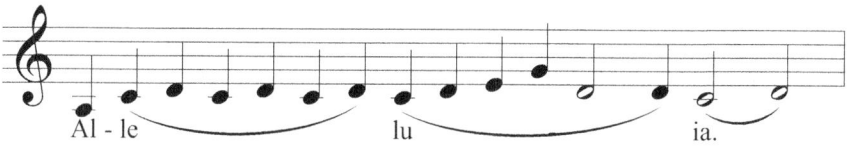

Al - le   lu   ia.

4

Neumes - Notes

■

Lord
A-men
Ho-san-na

One Pulse

One Syllable

(one part of a word)

Name: Punctum

■

Lord

■　　■

A - 　men

■　　■　　■

Ho - san - na

The punctum is the only note needed to write out any chant.

As we study we will find that the additional neumes and neume groupings that we are learning either:

1. Serve to tie a group of neumes together over one syllable

2. Indicate how to sing the neume

6

Length

Lord

A-men

Ho-san-na

Two Pulses
Two Syllables

Lord

■　■

A - men

■　　■　　■

Ho - san - na

A space between nuemes over one word tells us that each one is sung to a different syllable of the word.

8

Length

Lord
A-me
Ho-san-na

Two Pulses

One Syllable

■■

Lord

■　　■■

A -　　men

■　■■　■

Ho - san - na

Two neumes almost touching lengthen the amount of time
the syllable below is sung by the number of neumes above.

Chant notes are sung to an equal pulse, so distinctions we
make in modern music notation of whole notes, half notes,
eighth notes, sixteenth notes and their equivalent rests are
not needed. In modern music the neume would be a ♪ note,
two neumes close together a ♩ note.

Length

Lord
A-men
Ho-san-na

Three Pulses

One Syllable

∎∎∎

Lord

∎∎∎ ∎∎∎

A -   men

∎   ∎∎∎ ∎

Ho - san - na

This indicates the vowel is sung on one pitch for three pulses in what would be a dotted half-note ♩. in modern notation.

Decorations

Lord
A-men
Ho-san-na

Two Pulses
One Syllable

Also, at the end of a chant designates:

and is then called a Punctum Mora

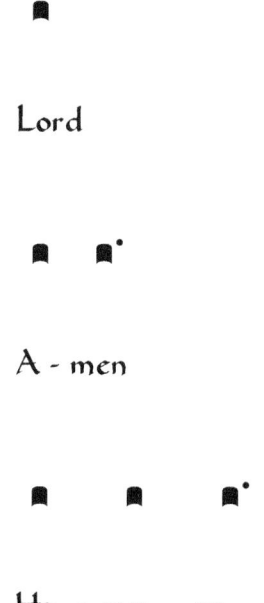

Lord

A - men

Ho - san - na

The dot indicates that this neume is interpreted in a special manner. This is the first "interpretation" chant sign we study. They may be called decorations.

This tells us to lengthen the neume to two pulses.

However, at the end of a chant this dot also means to soften the singing of the neume

14

Pitch

Lord
A-men
Ho-san-na

Two Pulses

One Syllable

Lord

A - men

Ho - san - na

Two notes touching are both sung to the same syllable.

They are always sung in order from left to right.

Pitch

Lord
A-men
Ho-san-na

Three Pulses

Three Syllables

Lord

A - men

Ho - san - na

Three notes not touching are sung in the direction they are arranged...rising or falling in pitch.

Pitch

_____

_____

_____

_____

Lord
A-men
Ho-san-na

No Pulses

No Syllables

Name: Staff

Lord

A - men

Ho - san - na

Each note is placed n a Staff. The Staff covers the natural range of the human voice, 9 pitches up and down. Notes may be placed on the spaces between lines and on the lines.

Occasionally an extra short line may be drawn in above or below the staff for permit the writing of a chant that goes beyond the usual range of the voice.

Pauses

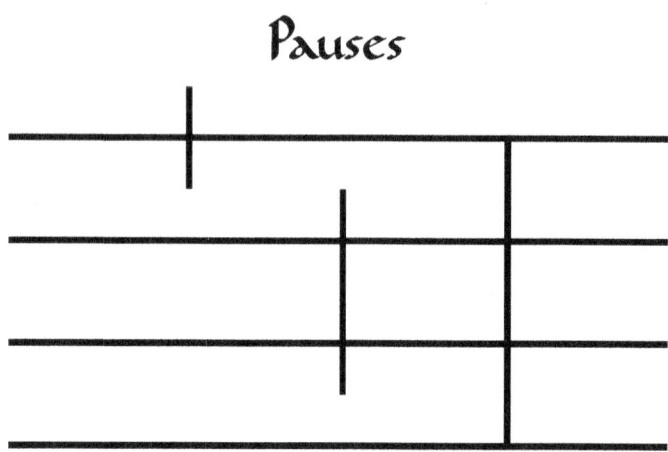

Lord
A-men
Ho-san-na

Quarter Line, No Break
Half and Full Line May Permit Breath

Lord

A - men

Ho - san - na

The pauses serve to break up the long lines of chant to make them easier to read and understand. The simple one cutting across one line has that purpose alone. The next two cutting through two lines or all four may also indicate that this is a place where a breath may be taken.

Pitch

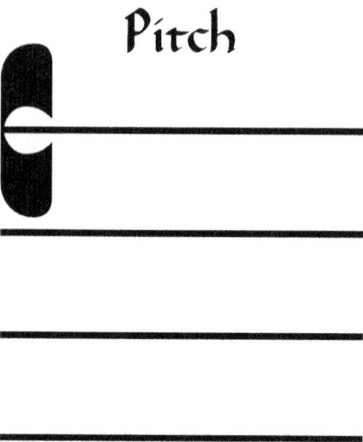

Lord
A-men
Ho-san-na

Name: DO Clef

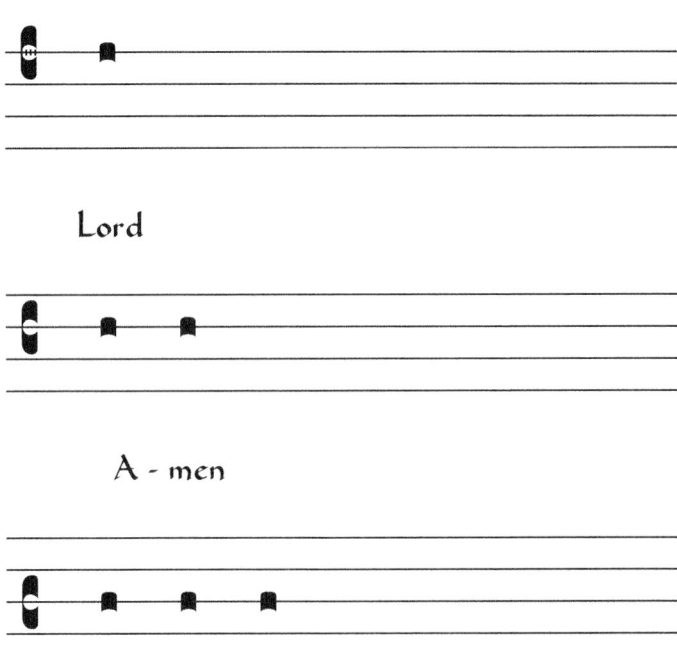

Lord

A - men

Ho - san - na

The DO may appear on just these three lines.

All the neumes above are the same pitch, DO.
This makes it possible to keep the notes of the melody cene-
tered on the four lines and three spaces of the staff.

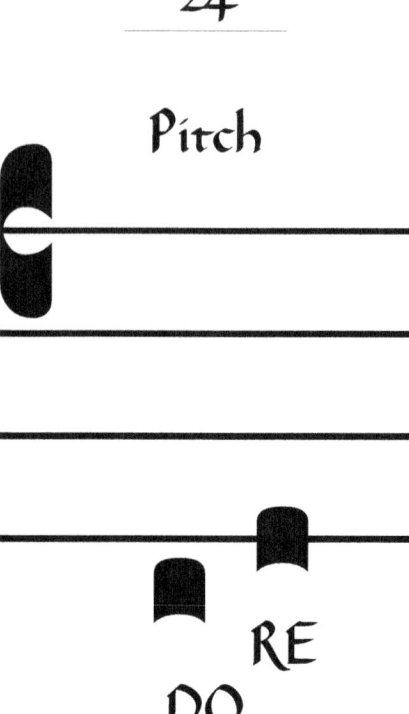

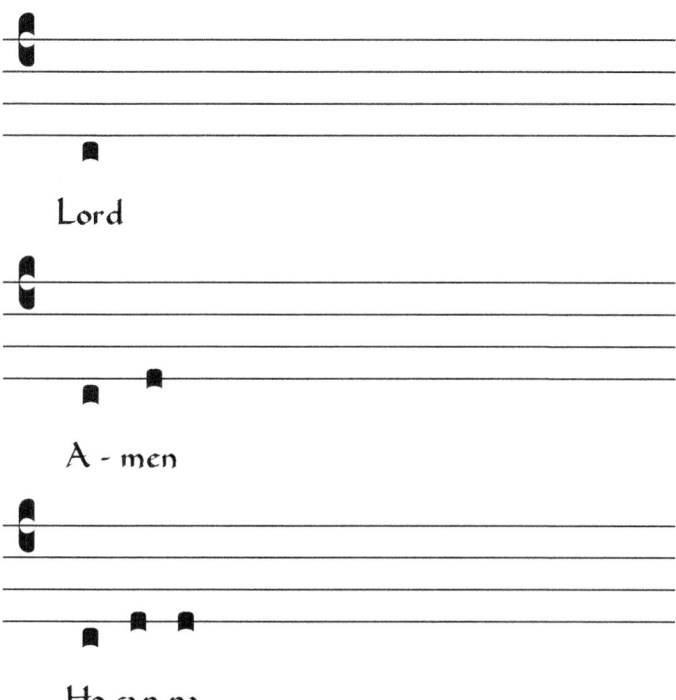

Lord

A - men

Ho san na

The first two intervals are DO and RE.

Pitch

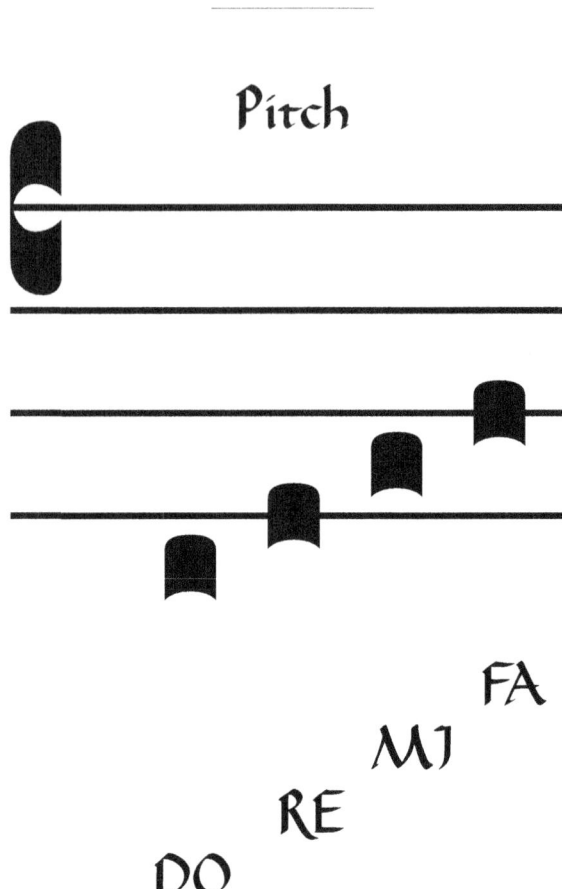

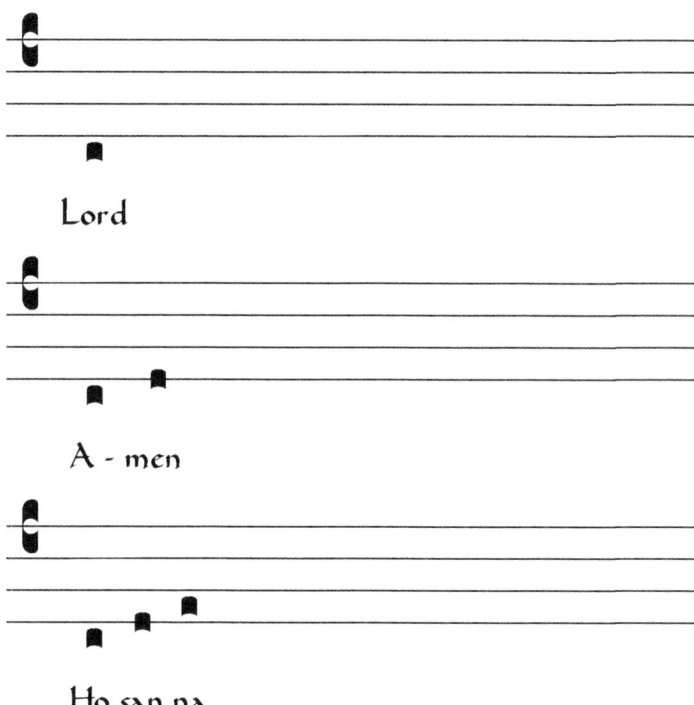

Lord

A - men

Ho san na

This is half of an octave stretching from DO to DO.. These neumes are evenly spaced in pitch until you reach the fourth. FA is half the pitch difference that you hear between DO, RE and MI.

This interval, the Perfect Fourth, in the building block of the octave.

Sing DO RE MI and then feel the urge to end on FA. MI "leads" you to FA. It's called a Leading Tone.

Pitch

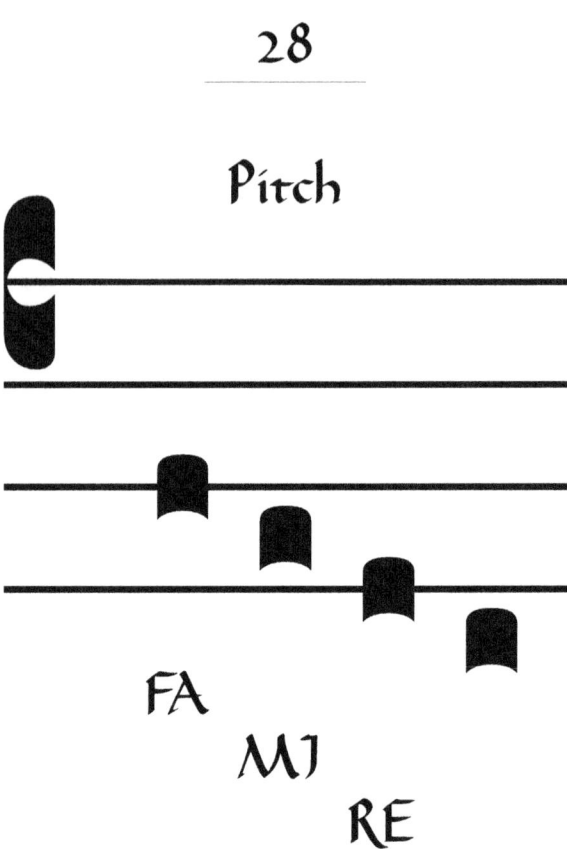

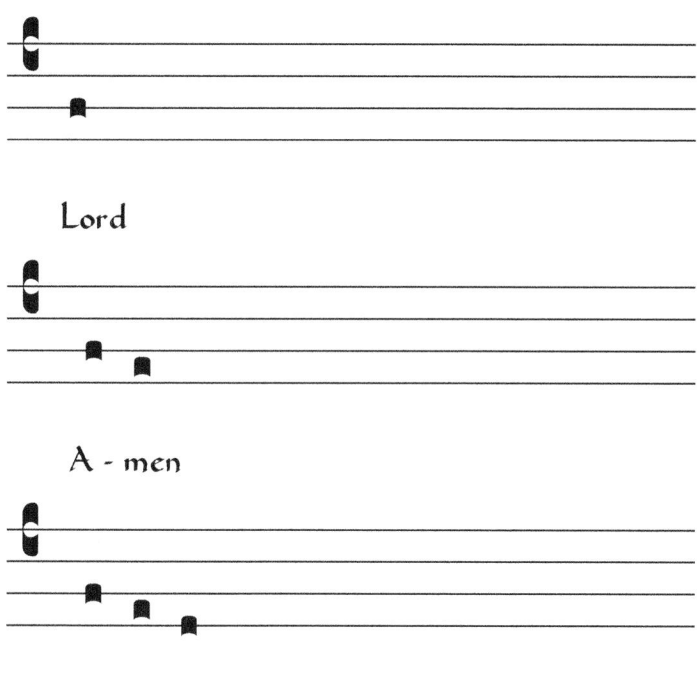

Lord

A - men

Ho san na

Singing down the scale of notes the effect of the FA - MI half-step is not as pronounced to the ear.

Composers of chant write whole-steps and half-steps in 8 different patterns called modes.

• Modern music uses only two modes commonly - that we call Major and Minor. Heavy emphasis on the TI DO is common, rarely do sections of pieces and endings ever not follow the TI DO pattern.

Pitch

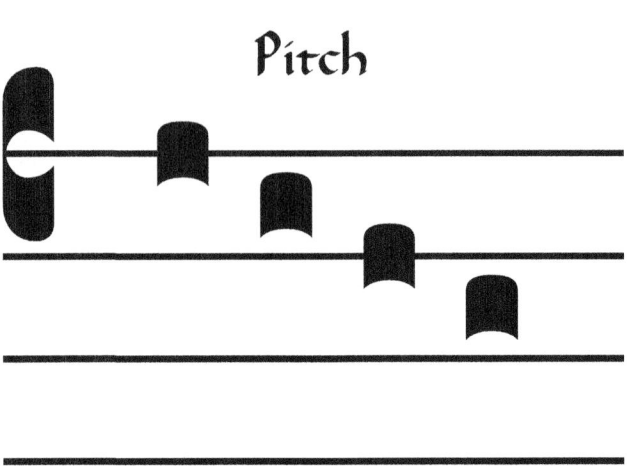

DO
TI
LA
SO

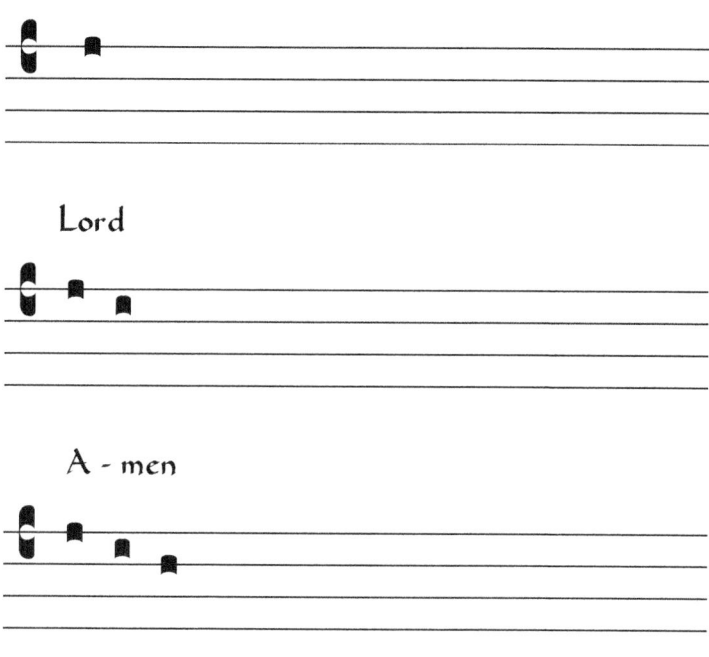

Lord

A - men

Ho san na

The second half of the octave is the second interval of four pitches that are stacked on top of the first set. to make an 8 note scale.

The Leading Tone here is TI. It's effect is not as pronouced here either as this is a descending scale.

Pitch

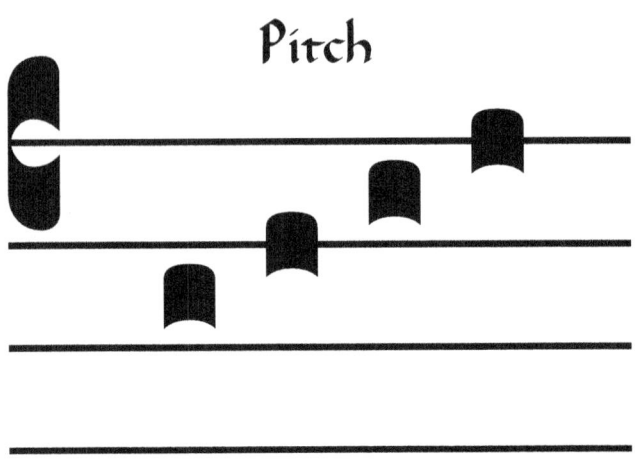

SO
LA
TI
DO

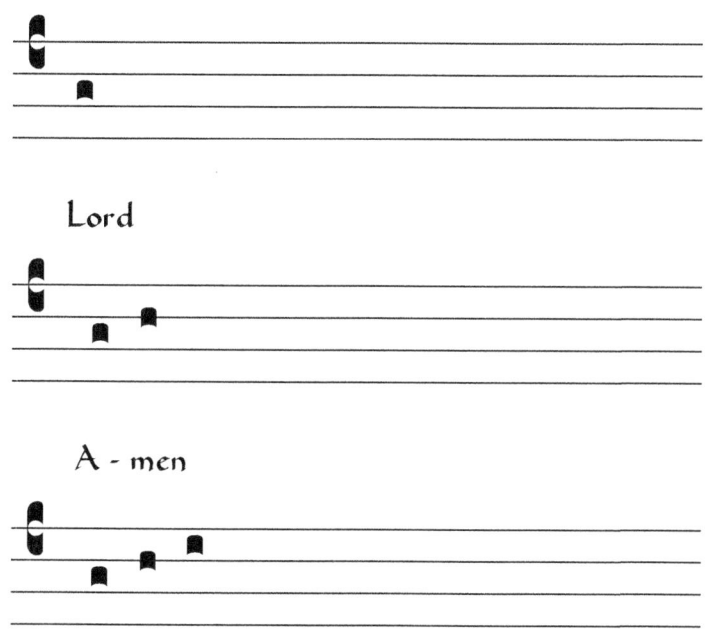

Lord

A - men

Ho san na

Here you will feel the pull from TI to resolve up to DO.

Pitch

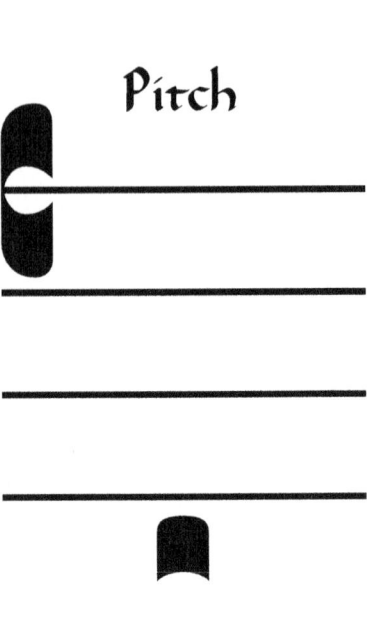

DO

Lord

A - men

Ho san na

Count down eighth positions (lines and spaces) of the staff from the DO Clef to find another DO an octave (8 notes) lower.

Pitch

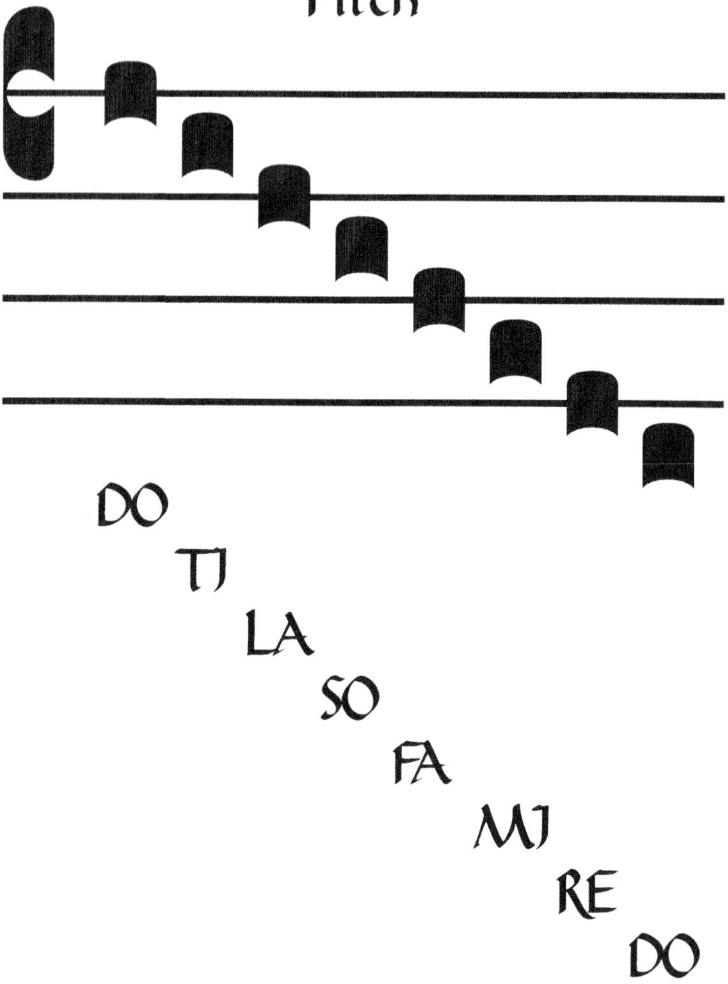

DO
TI
LA
SO
FA
MI
RE
DO

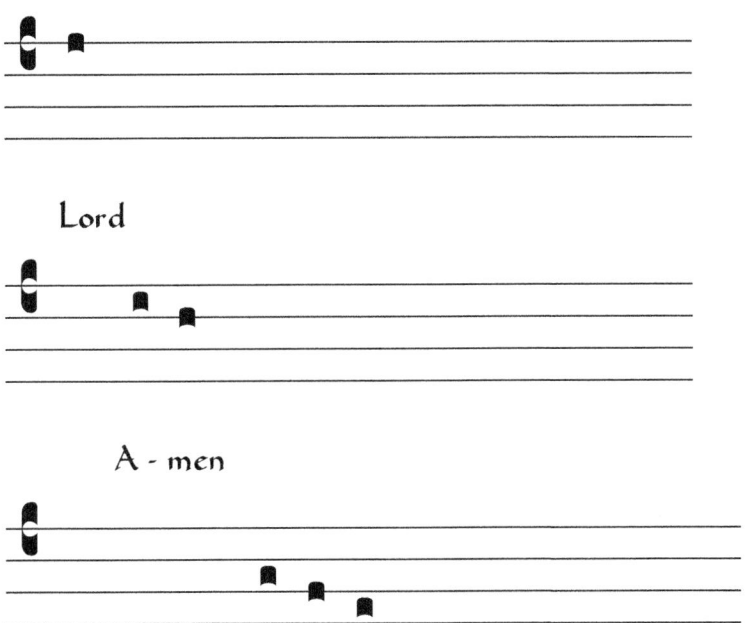

Lord

A - men

Ho san na

A full octave of pitches descending.

Pitch

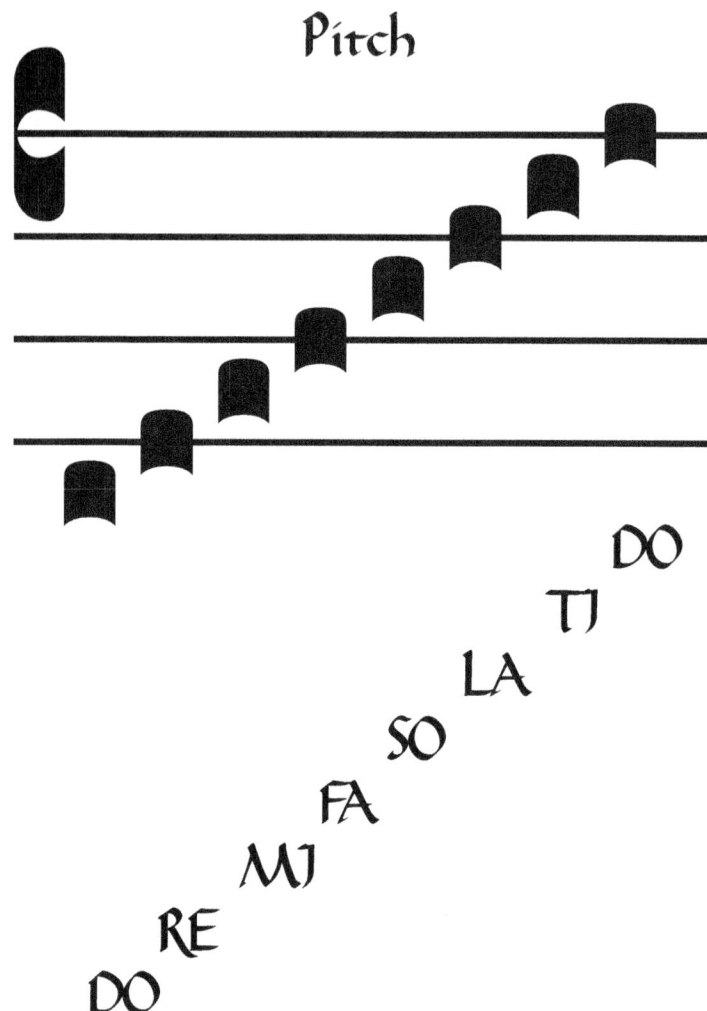

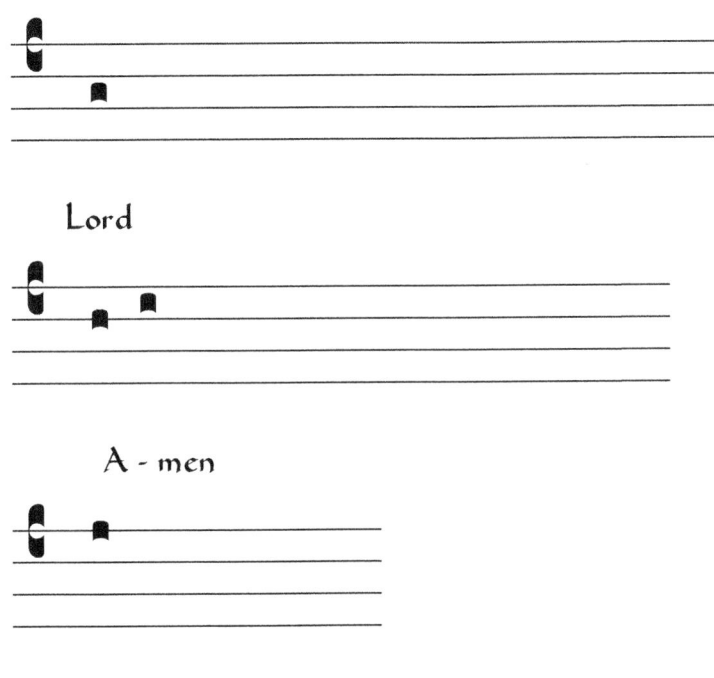

Lord

A - men

Ho san na

There are 8 Modes...that are used when writing chant melodies. Instead of ending on DO as many modern melodies do, chant melodies may begin and end on any note of the scale.

Some think this gives chant its "floating" character, as it is not bound to the modern major/minor tonality.

Music written from the time of Bach on all tends to only be in only two of the modes, what moderns call the Major and Minor.

Pitch

Lord
A-men
Ho-san-na

Two Pulses

One Syllable

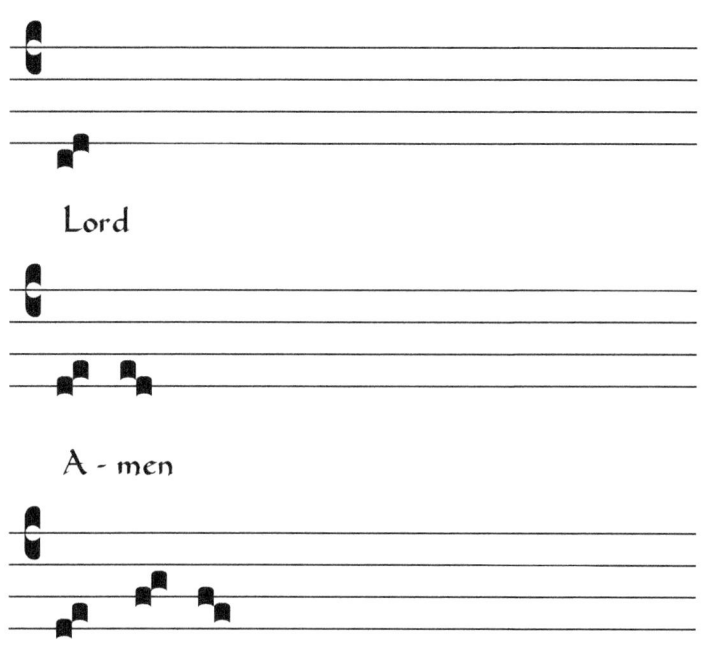

Lord

A - men

Ho - san - na

We review...two neumes sung on one syllable.

Pitch

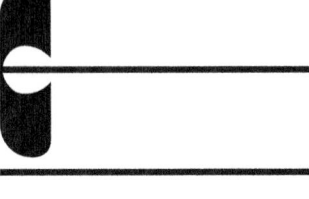

Lord
A-men
Ho-san-na

Two Pulses

Two Syllables

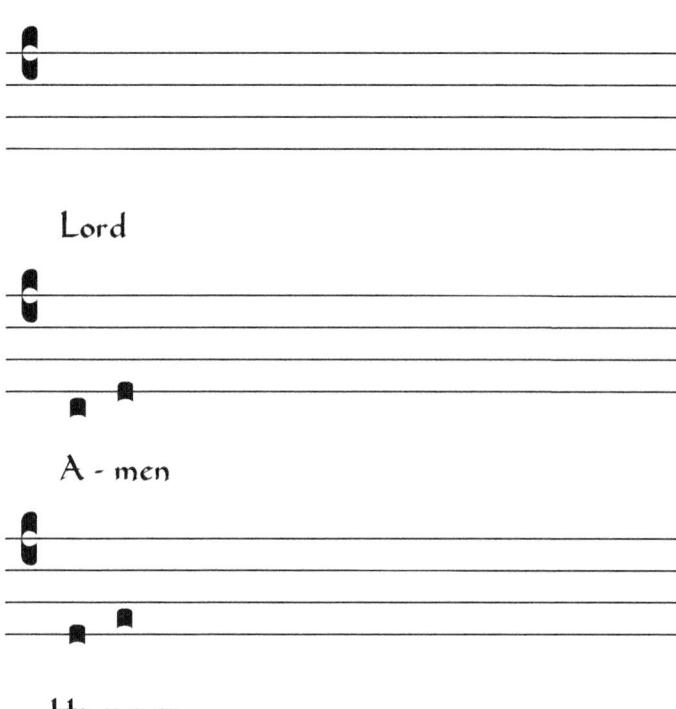

Lord

A - men

Ho san na

We review...one neume sung per one syllable.

The pulses that are the sung notes remain constant like the ticking of a clock.

In some editions space between neumes has a meaning. For more information about this, research Morea Vocis.

Pitch

Lord
A-men
Ho-san-na

Three Pulses

Three Syllables

Lord

A - men

Ho san na

Pitch

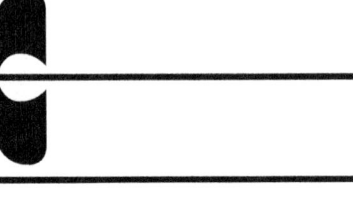

Lord
A-men
Ho-san-na

Three Pulses

One Syllable

Name: Torculus

Lord

A - men

Ho - san - na

The Torculus is one of the common neume arrangments that you will fin. When you see it, glance down, read the syllable, and then look up and sing the three neumes above it.

These neume combinations are like common road signs that trigger a response in the brain.

Pitch

Lord
A-men
Ho-san-na

One Pulse

One Syllable

Name: Virga

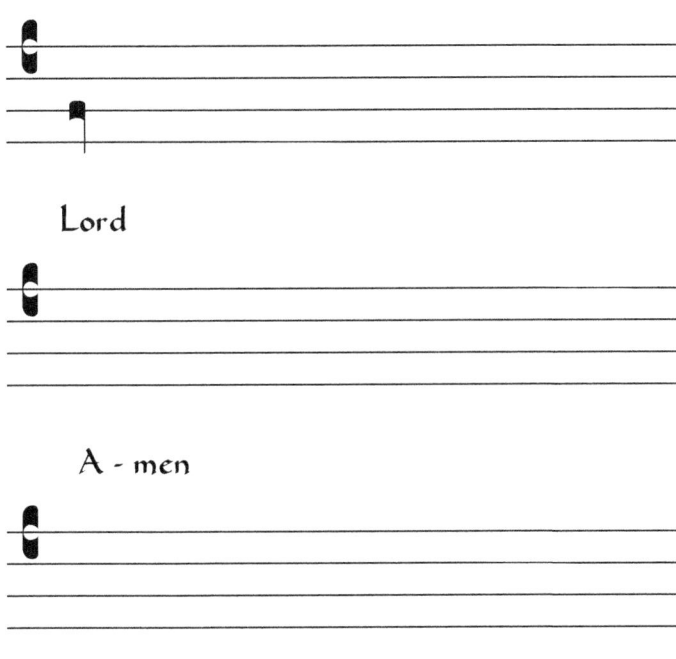

Lord

A - men

Ho - san - na

Note how the line on the Virga leads your eye.

It tells us the next neume we sing will be lower in pitch than this one.

Pitch

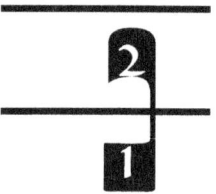

Lord
A-men
Ho-san-na

Two Pulses

One Syllable

Name: Podatus

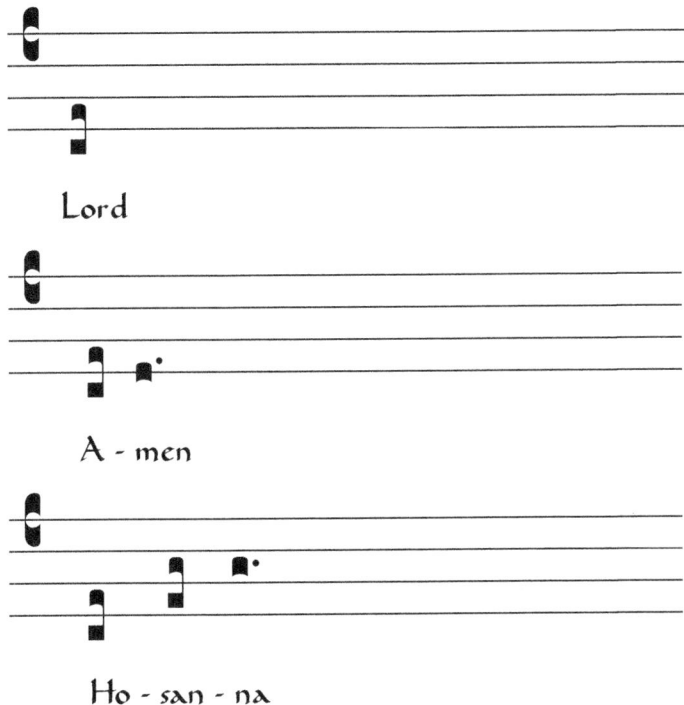

Lord

A - men

Ho - san - na

A line connects the two notes in this note configuration called Podatus or foot.

The lower note is sung first followed by the upper.

So our brain will understand we sing the same syllable on two notes, one lower and the next higher every time we see a Podatus. Podatus is "foot" in Latin.

Pitch

Lord
A-men
Ho-san-na

Two Pulses

One Syllable

Name: Clivis

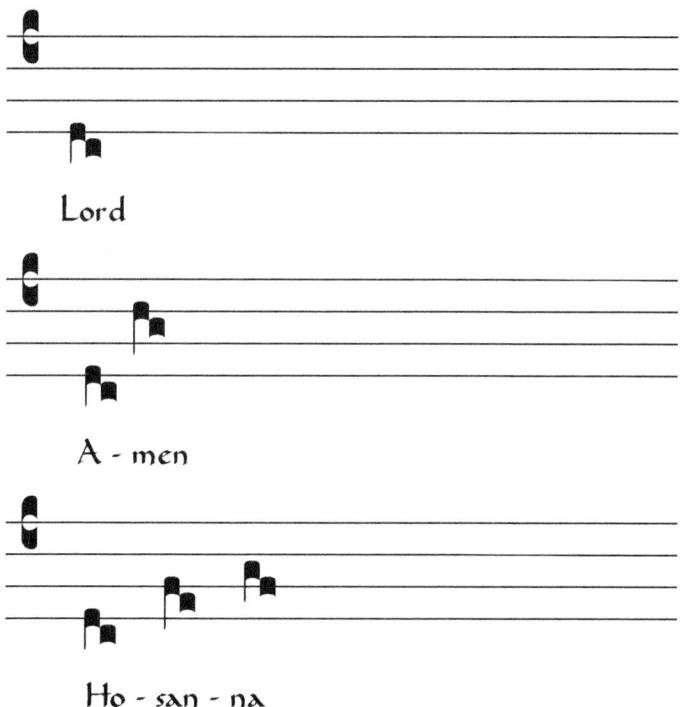

Lord

A - men

Ho - san - na

The Clivis starts with a vertical line that leads our eye to a higher pitch, almost always followed by a lower pitch.

Pitch

Lord
A-men
Ho-san-na

Three Pulses

One Syllable

Name: Punctum Inclinatum

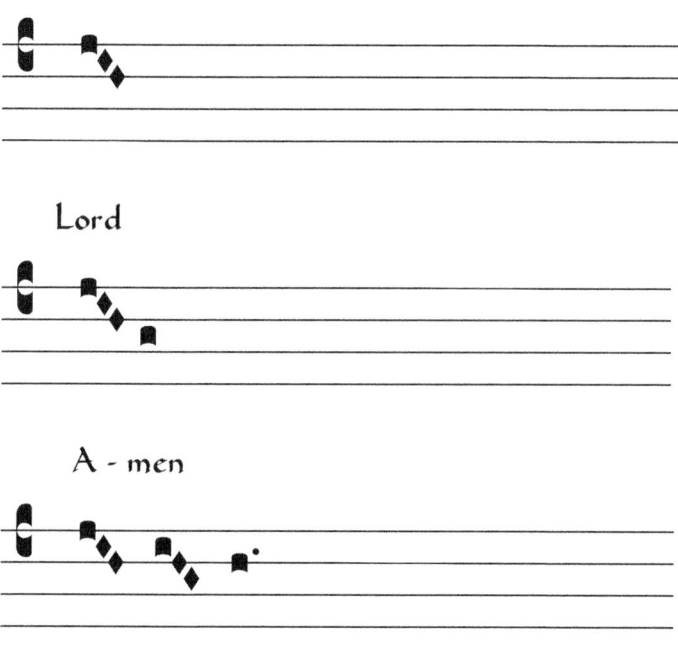

Lord

A - men

Ho - san - na

The Inclinatum is a dead give-away that we are singing more than one pitch on a syllable.

As you may have already discovered, while all of the forms of neumes we have seen could be represented by individual neumes strung across a page, the clumping of them in structured forms gives us a heads up and simplifies the reading of chant.

Pitch

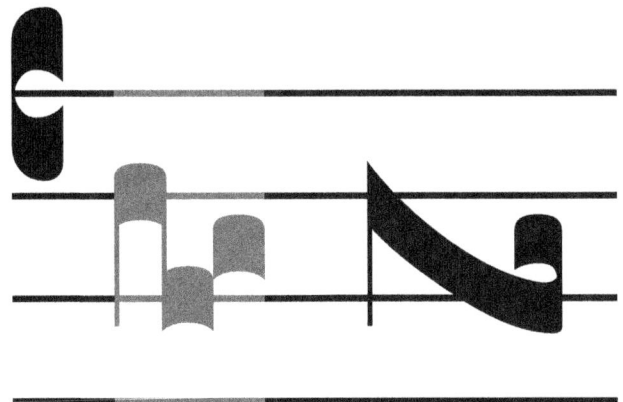

Lord
A-men
Ho-san-na

Three Pulses

One Syllable

Name: Porrectus

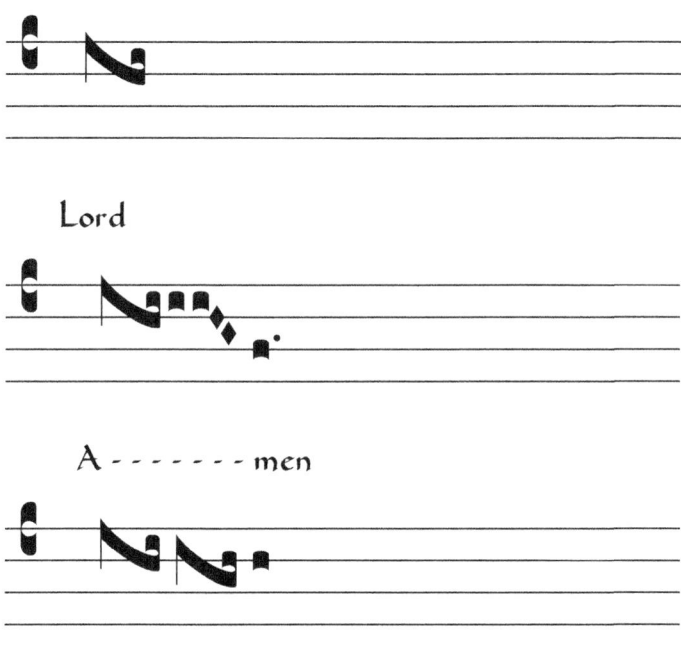

Lord

A - - - - - - - men

Ho - san - na

For some the most difficult of neumes to read, it's simply an easy way to write a group of three neumes that follow a pitch pattern of high, low and back to mid.

The grey notes on the left page shows the same notes that are in the Porrectus that follows it.

It was easier for those writing chant to write without lifting the pen from the score than three neumes. And it clearly defines a unique yet common musical pitch pattern.

Pitch

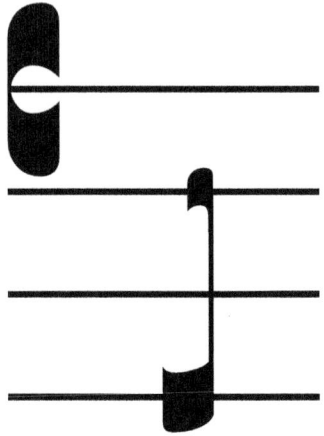

Lord
A-men
Ho-san-na

Two Pulses

One Syllable

Name: Liquescent

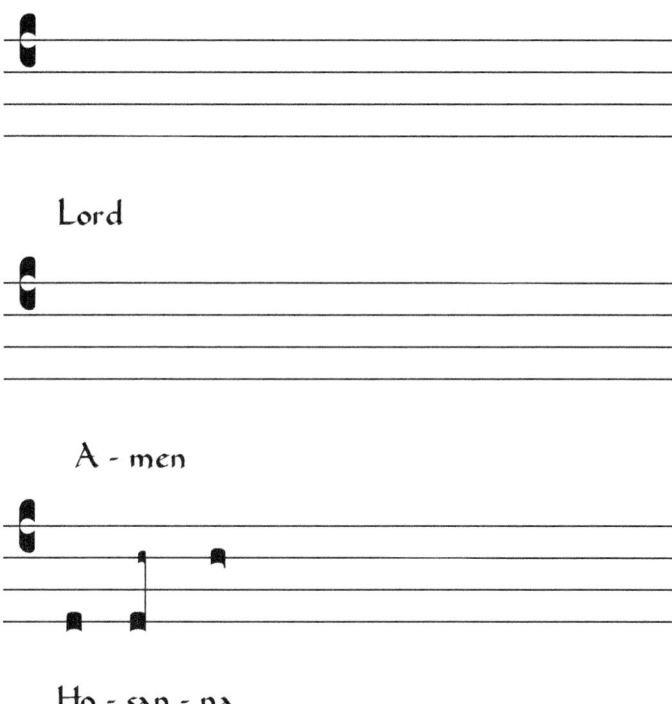

Lord

A - men

Ho - san - na

The tiny note of the Liquescent is always a consonant that may resonate when sung....quietly.

Think Sa Ahn. Say it, let your tongue flip to the roof of your mouth to make the soft AHN sound.

Modern Decoration

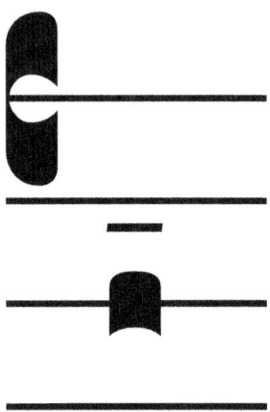

Lord
A-men
Ho-san-na

A Lengthened Pulse

One Syllable

Name: Horizontal Episema

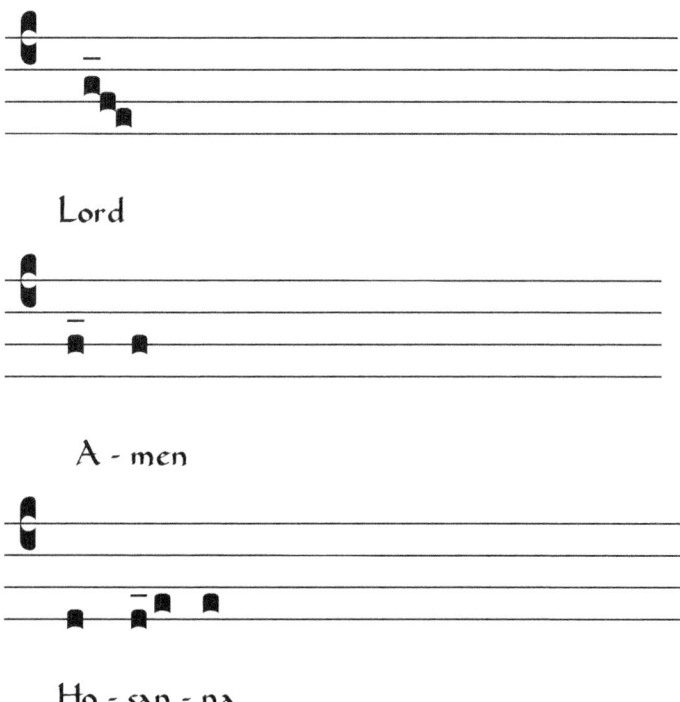

Lord

A - men

Ho - san - na

Emphasis, usually thought to be stretching of the neume in time.

Just one of the additions made to more modern chant notation to more fully guide us in the interpretation of chant.

These signs were created and added to chant in response to a desire to try and write down the musical things that were sung and passed down as tradition.

Modern Decoration

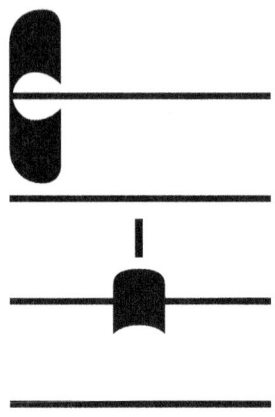

Lord
A-men
Ho-san-na

Indicates initial note of 2 or 3 note group

Name: Vertical Episema

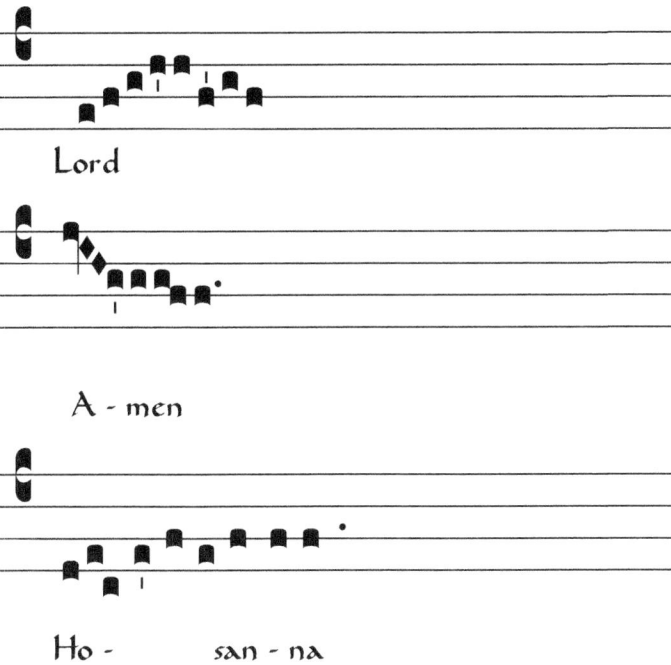

Lord

A - men

Ho -   san - na

Just one of the additions made to chant notation to more
fully explain interpretation.

The Monks of the Abbey of Solesmes were charged with the
mission of further editing chant to assist those singing in un-
derstanding the underlying rhythm...groups of two and three
neumes, that are the heart and soul of chant. They used the
vertical mark shown to point out the Ictus.

Pitch

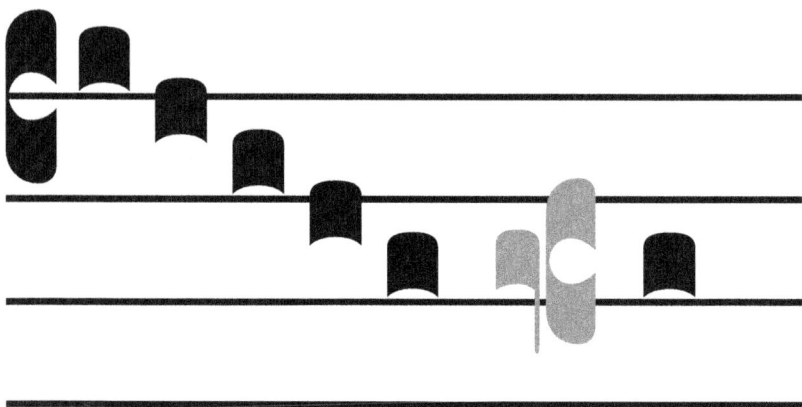

DO
TI
LA
SO
FA   FA

Do and Fa Clefs Center melody on Staff

Name: FA Clef

Pitch

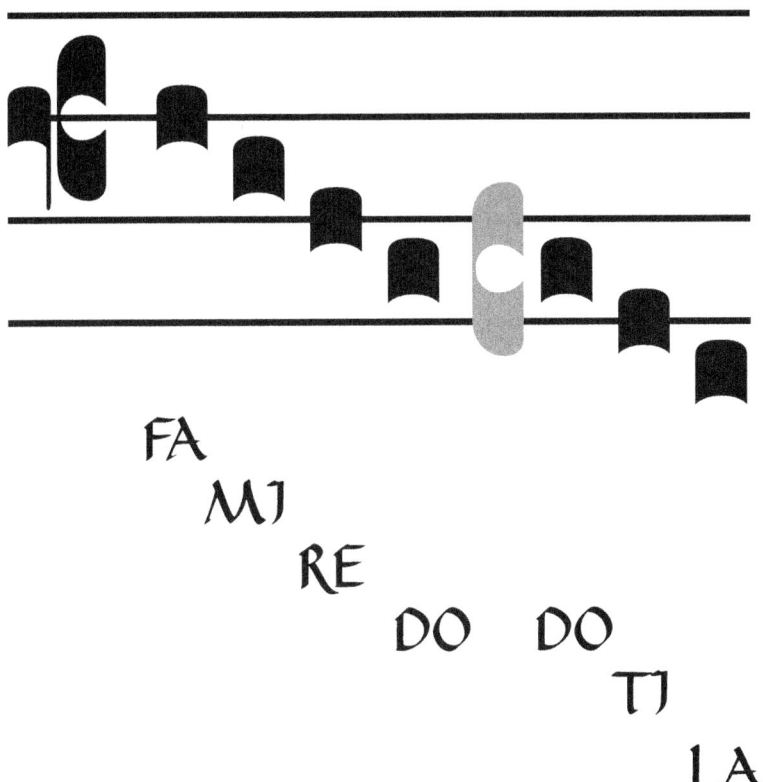

Pitch

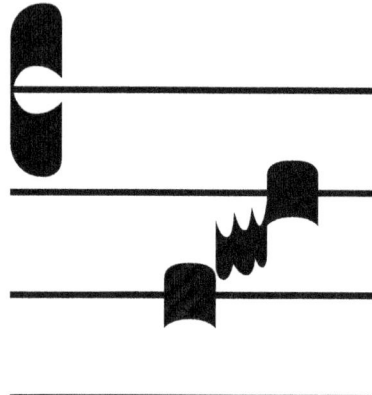

Lord
A-men
Ho-san-na

One Syllable

Name: Quilisma

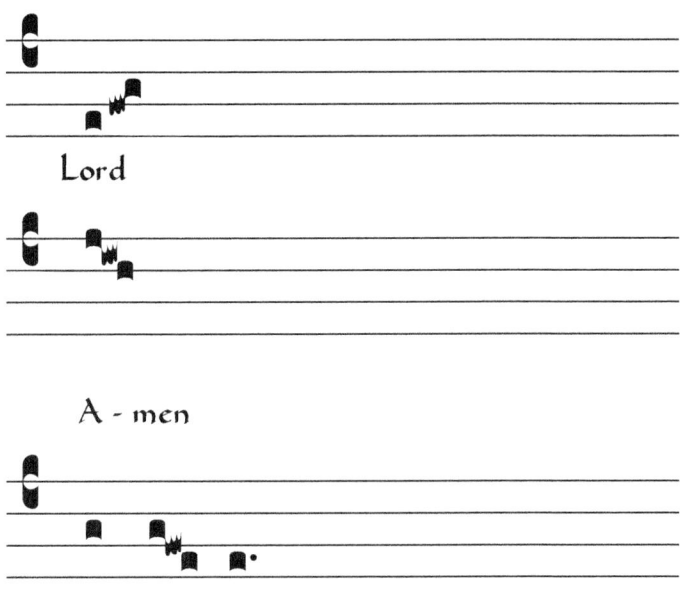

Lord

A - men

Ho - san - na

It is generally accepted that the squiggle indicates that the note prior to it is sung as a lengthened note.

Pitch

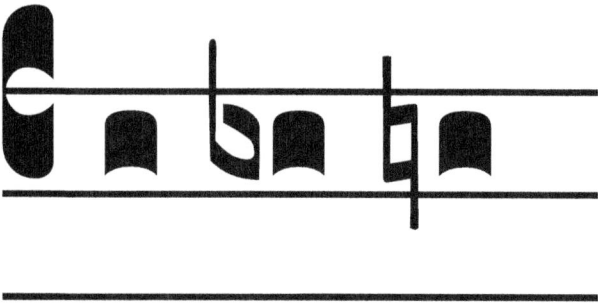

TJ   TE   TJ

Flat lowers TJ one-half step to TE

Natural resets it back to TJ.

It only appears on the pitch TJ.

Name: Flat & Natural

Pitch

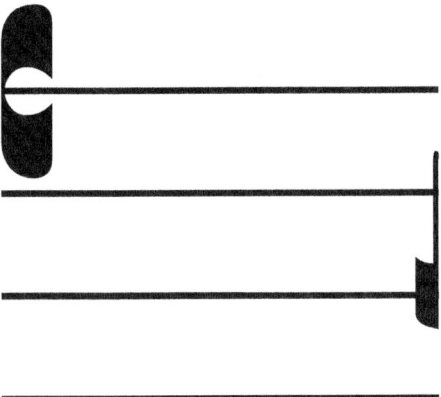

Lord
A-men
Ho-san-na

Silent - Not Sung

Indicates First Note coming up to be sung

on next Lower Staff

Name: Custos

Definitions

Clivis	Higher note comes first in group of two
Custos	Indicates next pitch on next staff.
Divisions	Ends of phrases and lines where breaths may be taken.
DO Clef	Shows location of DO on Staff.
FA Clef	Shows location of FA on Staff
Flat	Pitch of TI is lowered to TE, a half-step.
Ictus	First "lift" note in groups of two or three.
Inclinatum	A note that is leaning rather than straight.
Natural	Raises Flatted TE back up to TI.
Neumes	Notes
Podatus	"Foot", the basic neume or note.
Porrectus	High note then lower note and high note
Punctum	"Point", a single note or neume
Inclinatum	A note that is leaning rather than straight.
Punctum Mora	A note that is longer and dies away.
Quilisma	Three notes, first lengthened.
Repercussive	The same syllable sung more than once on same pitch
Staff	Four Lines
Torculus	Opposite of Porrectus
Virga	Descending notes

MASS XI, *Orbis factor*

K Y-ri- e * e- lé- i-son. *iij.* Chri-ste

e- lé- i-son. *iij.* Ký-ri- e e- lé- i- son. *ij.*

Ký- ri- e * e- lé- i-son.

G Ló- ri- a in excélsis De- o. Et in terra pax

homí-ni-bus bonæ vo- luntá- tis. Laudámus te. Be-ne-

dí- cimus te. Ado-rámus te. Glo- ri-fi-cámus te.

Grá-ti- as á-gimus ti-bi propter magnam gló- ri- am tu- am.

Dómi- ne De- us, Rex cæ-lé-stis, De- us Pa-ter omní- pot-

ens. Dómi- ne Fi- li u-ni-gé-ni-te Je- su Chri-ste,

Dómi-ne De-us, Agnus De-i, Fí-li-us Pa-tris. Qui

tol-lis peccá-ta mun-di, mi-se-ré-re no-bis. Qui tol-lis

peccá-ta mun-di, súsci-pe depreca-ti-ó-nem nostram. Qui

se-des ad déx-te-ram Pa-tris, mi-se-ré-re no-bis. Quóni-am

tu so-lus sanctus. Tu so-lus Dómi-nus. Tu so-lus Altís-

simus, Je-su Chri-ste. Cum Sancto Spí-ri-tu, in gló-

ri-a De-i Pa-tris. A-men.

These two sample chant pages are used with permission of the
Church Music Association of America. They are pages from The
Parish Book of Chant. We highly recommend this book for your
schola, choir and congregation.

Vist the CMAA website at: www.musicasacra.com.

Noel Jones first sang chant in a choir of men and boys and followed that up by chanting daily masses before he was a teenager in a small town in Ohio.

Summer studies with Benedictine monks took him further along the chant path prior to his leaving for New York City where he directed Catholic choirs and was organist at the Church Center for the United Nations as well as accompanist for the United Nations Singers. Later in Germany he was organist for the English masses at the DOM Cathedral in Frankfurt.

Working as a chor-repetiteur in Germany he was involved in vocal coaching as well as a musical direction in Frankfurt, Berlin, Hamburg, Bremen and Munich. Of the three Broadway musicals he led there, he conducted two recordings and the European premiere of one. Having experience setting translations to scores, he was engaged to do so in Germany, the United States and eventually Italy, where he set the Italian text for Sir William Walton's opera The Bear. He also served as chor repetiteur and rehearsal conductor for that performance under the supervision of Sir William.

During this time he played for masses at Il Duomo in Barga, Italy, as well as producing and conducting the town's annual San Cristoforo Day celebration concert in the 11th century church.

Working as a church organ designer , he eventually located in Tennessee, where he joined the staff of a Catholic church as director of music involved in returning church music to chant and polyphony. He along with Mary C. Weaver have founded Musicam Sacram, a CMAA chapter in East Tennesee.

His books are edited by Ellen Doll Jones, his wife, who is an active organist choir director and recitalist.

.

The Pulse of Music

Book 1
A Beginner's Guide
To Reading
Gregorian Chant Notation

Book 2
A Beginner's Guide
To Singing
Gregorian Chant Rhythm and Solfeggio

Books 1&2 Combined
A Beginner's Guide
to Singing Gregorian Chant
Notation, Rhythm and Solfeggio

Gregorian Chant Blank Staff Notebook

A Gregorian Chant Coloring Book
for Children & Adults
Student Edition • Teacher's Edition

If you can sing "Joy to the World"
you can learn to read and sing Gregorian Chant
For People Who Can And Cannot Read Music.

The Catholic Choir Book Series
www.thecatholicchoirbook.com

The Catholic Hymnal
www.thecatholichymnalcom

Frog Music Press
201 County Road 432 • Englewood, TN 37329 • 423 887-7594

Printed in Great Britain
by Amazon

12121170R00047